KAREN CAMPBELL

skin tone
SECRETS

MARKER EDITION

The **ULTIMATE** Guide
for Creating a Vast Array of Distinctly Gorgeous
and Perfectly Blended Skin Tones in Alcohol Markers!

A Quick Note From The Author...

This book is dedicated to all my Art Club students at Awesome Art School who get creative with and draw alongside me (albeit virtually) every day! It's YOU (and your amazing, developing talents!!) who inspire me to continue keepin' on as I do! Keep up the fabulous drawing, my friends, and never forget that YOU CAN'T GET WORSE with more practice; that's not a thing!!! So grab your markers and let's DO THIS!

To watch a free video that shares my best alcohol marker coloring & blending tips on YouTube go to: https://bit.ly/bestmarkertips

Text and Illustrations Copyright © 2022 by Karen Campbell. All rights reserved.
Author, Illustrator, Publisher: Karen Campbell, Artist, LLC karencampbellartist.com
Cover Design: KT Design, LLC ktdesignllc.com
Editors: Linda Duvel

This book has been written and designed to aid the aspiring artist. Reproduction of work for at-home practice is permissible. Any art produced, electronically reproduced, or distributed from this publication for commercial purposes is forbidden without written content from the publisher, Karen Campbell, Artist, LLC. If you would like to use material from this book for any purpose outside of private use, prior written permission must be obtained by contacting the publisher at karen@awesomeartschool.com. Thank you for supporting the author's rights. Lastly, this book is NOT sponsored by any companies mentioned in this book. All opinions expressed and art materials shown are my own.

TABLE OF CONTENTS

ALL ABOUT MARKERS 4

PAPER 9

PRO COLORING TIPS 10

CREATING LOVELY SKIN TONES 12

HAIR RENDERING TECHNIQUES 20

SHADING & LIGHT SOURCES 25

HIGHLIGHTS 27

WHAT NOT TO USE WITH MARKERS 28

COLOR SELECTIONS 29

HOW TO USE THIS BOOK 30

SECTION 1 SKIN TONES 35

SECTION 2 SKIN TONES 47

SECTION 3 SKIN TONES 59

FREEBIES FOR YOU 72

LET'S CONNECT 73

MORE FUN ART BOOKS 74

WHY MARKERS?

Quite simply, markers make coloring super duper fun!
They are also easy to use, widely available worldwide, extremely portable, make coloring FAST and come in a HUGE range of vibrant color choices and ink types.
There are 5 main types of markers.

PAINT-BASED

Paint markers are just that: markers that contain permanent, lightfast, acrylic or oil-based paint. These types of markers are PERFECT for adding pops of highlights and opaque marks and lines for almost any mixed media application or art/craft project. There are many brands of paint pens/markers available. Uni-Posca is my favorite brand as they come in a large range of colors and have many nib varieties to choose from.

PIGMENT-BASED

Pigment-based markers are also fabulous. The ink inside is also permanent, lightfast and their richly pigmented inks also apply opaquely. These are also excellent for mixed media applications. Faber-Castell makes my favorite called the PITT artist pen (as shown).

DYE-BASED

Dye-based markers are found everywhere and are in every craft store. They are generally the cheapest and come in lots of fun, vibrant colors. The ink inside these is typically transparent and is not lightfast, meaning they will fade with time and exposure to sunlight. These are super fun as the ink inside is also water-soluble. What does that mean? It means that when you add water to your marks, they melt into a watercolor-like effect!

WATERCOLOR

Watercolor markers work in the same way that dye-based markers do except that they are extremely lightfast and are typically MORE reactive to water than dye-based markers as the ink inside is of a higher quality. Winsor & Newton is my favorite brand as they are very juicy and come in fun colors! Unfortunately they come with a higher price tag too.

WHAT ABOUT ALCOHOL MARKERS?

Alcohol markers are unique in that the pigments (the tiny color particles) are suspended in an alcohol solution rather than in a dye-based, water-based or oil-based liquid like all the other markers.

They can be layered in a sophisticated way to produce almost painterly effects!

Here's how they work:

When an alcohol marker is applied to a non-porous surface (or not-super-absorbant paper like Bristol) the alcohol solution stays wet for a few moments.

If you touch your paper at this point, you'll notice it feels cold! That's because it's still wet from the solution.

A drawing done in alcohol markers. Taken from my **Whimsical Women of the World Book**, published in 2021

After a few seconds the alcohol itself evaporates, the paper dries (and interestingly warms up) and what remains behind on the paper is just the pigment (or color) itself. That's the color you see! Cool, right?

Well, what's even cooler is that when subsequent layers are added, the solution from the top layers acts to re-wet some of the pigments underneath, and then blending occurs!

The result? Well, it can be very much like painting, both the process and the colors left behind!!

But, while this seems easy, there are some tricks that can help you out greatly as it's harder than it seems, unfortunately. Luckily all my tips in this book will help you, so turn the page and I'll share my best ones with you now.

ANATOMY OF A MARKER

This book will focus on alcohol markers and how to create amazing skin tones with them!

As such, the way we color with them, not just WHAT the colors are, but HOW we use the marker itself, will have a great impact on our results.

So first, we need to get to know our markers! All of these little details matter and soon you'll see why!

CHISEL NIB

Pretty much all large barrelled alcohol markers will have one end that has a chisel nib. I only use this end about 5% of the time. All other work is done with the brush nib.

BRANDS

There are LOTS of brands that make alcohol markers.
Luckily the inks in all of them work the same way, so choose any brand you like. What's most important is that they have a brush nib and how much they cost. Copics are the gold standard in alcohol markers. But they cost a fortune (about $8/marker).

BARREL REFILLABLE?

The middle of the marker is called the barrel. That's what's holding all the ink inside. Some alcohol markers (like Copics) are refillable. Most are not. Other companies (like Ohuhu) claim they will be making refillable versions soon. I hope that this is true!! To refill the ink simply pull off the nib and you can pour the refill directly into the barrel.

BRUSH NIB

I do 95% of coloring using this nib.
Be careful when selecting alcohol markers online. Typically the least expensive markers do NOT have a brush nib on one end. They will have a chisel on one side and a tiny nib (called a "bullet" nib) on the other.
Definitely find one that has a brush nib!

WHAT WE WILL BE USING

I cannot lie. Copics are my favorite alcohol markers! I have collected all 300+ colors of them! BUT, due to their high cost, I never recommend them to my dear students; that just seems too cruel. However, as I've stated before, there are many many alternatives on the market. So which ones do I recommend instead?

I really love the Ohuhu brand. And I think they've done the best "Copic replica" of any brand out there (and I've pretty much sampled them all at this point). And at $1/marker, I can feel good about making that recommendation to you and to my students at Awesome Art School.

vs.

This 36 piece skin tone set of Ohuhu markers retails at $39 on Amazon at the time of publication.
This is the set I'll exclusively be swatching and working with throughout this book.

This 6 piece skin tone set of Copic markers retails at $36 on Amazon at the time of publication. Ouch.

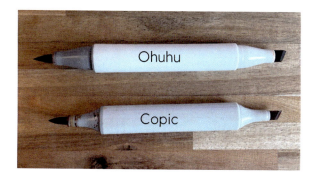

Important Note:
Ohuhu also sells a 24 set of Skin Tones and also has sets that do NOT have the brush nib (instead they have the chisel/bullet combo). So choose carefully when ordering online!

As you can see, both markers are very similar. Both have a chisel nib on one end and a brush nib on the other. I still feel the Copics brush nib and ability to refill make it a superior marker but Ohuhu is plenty good enough and, at a fraction of the price, I still highly recommend them!

MORE TIPS!

Test, test, test and test some more. Before you start coloring, check the marker color on a separate piece of scratch paper. Marker cap colors are notorious for not being a true representation of the actual color.

Here's a perfect example of why testing is so important. This color by Ohuhu is called Black Brown. The swatch looks orange and the cap looks yellow-y to me in person. What the heck? TEST SO YOU KNOW for SURE what you're getting when you dive into a project. NO one likes a surprise when you're trying to be so careful. With that in mind, just because I swatch all the colors of the Ohuhu 36 Skin Tone set in this book, does not mean you shouldn't still swatch them all for yourself.

As I'm sure you may be aware, the scanning and printing process alters the true colors of alcohol marker prints so what you see in this book may in fact look quite different from what you see in person.

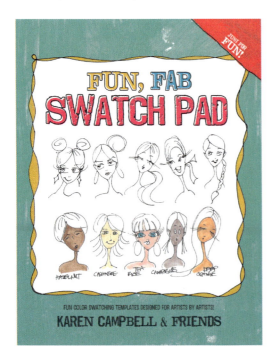

If swatching tiny squares seems boring to you, I highly recommend my Fun Fab Swatch Pad. It makes swatching FUN!

And if you're wondering how to draw your own faces just like the ones you see me color in this book, check out the entire fun fab drawing series to learn how to draw your own!

  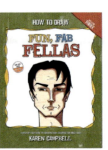

PAPER IS EVERYTHING

Paper is **AS IMPORTANT** as the markers you're using and I'm in no way exaggerating here!

My favorite paper is Smooth Bristol, but it's expensive. As always, I'm conscious of my students' wallets, so I usually recommend a very inexpensive alternative (Hammermill, shown below, right) that you can buy from Amazon or most office supply stores. For printing at home, I suggest any cardstock that is less than 70 lbs.

You can find links to all my favorite art supplies at
www.amazon.com/shop/karencampbellartist

I know that marker paper is "a thing" and I've bought it many times to test it out. I personally do not care for it as it is very thin and transparent. It is also expensive! Definitely feel free to skip if you spot it in your nearest art or crafts store!

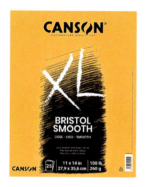
Smooth Bristol is the best choice but rather expensive.

This is my favorite - I LOVE this paper! Unfortunately, it doesn't work in my printer so I use it only for drawing.

This paper is not as smooth BUT it works with my at-home printer so I can print out drawings for coloring practice.

I recommend the **Ohuhu 36 Skin Tone Set** of alcohol markers. This is the set I will be using throughout this book. You can refer to the swatches of each color on the following pages to get a good sense of the color variation within the pack. As you can see, there's a nice range of light to dark.

If you choose to get this set, remember to swatch them out on YOUR own paper too, as colors can vary due to the printing process. If you have yet to try these, you're in for a treat! They're great and I just know you'll love them!

Marker Coloring Pro-Tips

The First Layer

First, you need to color quickly and at a constant/consistent pace. The best blending occurs when the layers are still nice and wet. Alcohol markers dry pretty quickly so you need to move fast if you want them to blend.

On this sample I changed up when I was going fast and then slow. My marks look COMPLETELY different from one another, even though I did it all at one time.

On this one I moved consistently. While it's still pretty streaky (we will get to that next) at least the lines are more or less the same.

Eliminating Streaks

To help "fix" streaks, work systematically in two directions. Do the first layer in one direction (or do small circles). Then do a second layer, making your strokes in the opposite direction.

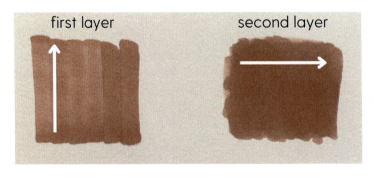

See? No more streaks :)

However, you may not like the fact that your square is now a darker color than you had originally intended. We can fix that too (everything is fixable, if not preventable!).

To make the area look the SAME (only no streaks) do the second layer in a color that is ONE SHADE LIGHTER than the first. Doing the same color twice will DARKEN the appearance of that color. Turn the page to see just what I mean...

FIXING STREAKS WHILE RETAINING ORIGINAL COLOR

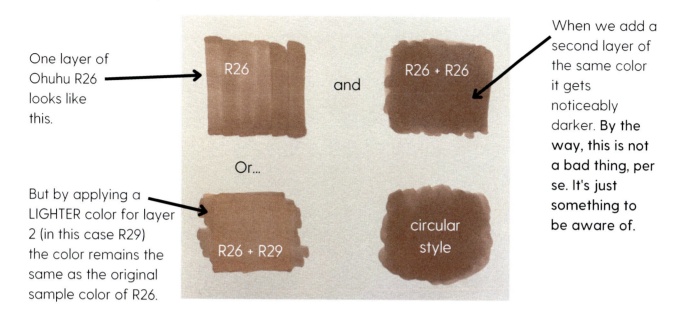

One layer of Ohuhu R26 looks like this.

When we add a second layer of the same color it gets noticeably darker. **By the way, this is not a bad thing, per se. It's just something to be aware of.**

But by applying a LIGHTER color for layer 2 (in this case R29) the color remains the same as the original sample color of R26.

Some people prefer to work in small circular motions. That is also a great choice and the same concept applies. For whatever reason, I love lines. Each to his/her own. It's all good!

THE COLORLESS BLENDER - SKIP IT

Important: Do NOT use the colorless blender. That only results in the **lightening** of the original pigment color and often causes even more streaking woes. It simply dilutes the colors you have down already. Always use a **colored** marker of some shade when you layer and remember: go LIGHTER by one shade to stay the same as the original color.

A colored marker does a far better job at blending as the pigments from the two markers are NEEDED to work together to mix. That's how blending works!

Continue on to see ALL 36 of the colors included in the Ohuhu Skin Tone Set. Then we will discuss just how to create those lovely tones!

Creating Lovely Skin Tones

Okay, so now that we have some layering and blending basics down, let's apply this to skin tones! I've already gone ahead and done all the hard work for you by picking the colors that go best together. The following pages will give you the best combos to use! Just pick one and color with confidence!!!

Before we go there, however, I thought it'd be worth learning how to blend them together awesomely so they look natural on your face drawings!

You'll also see that I've laid these steps out on each and every sample page, but let's do a deep dive, right here, so you're crystal clear on each step and so you can see it on a larger scale.

I'll also show you, in detail, some of the finishing steps that will surely help bring your characters to life: like how to render hair, and where to apply all the fun dabs of highlights!

Let's do this!

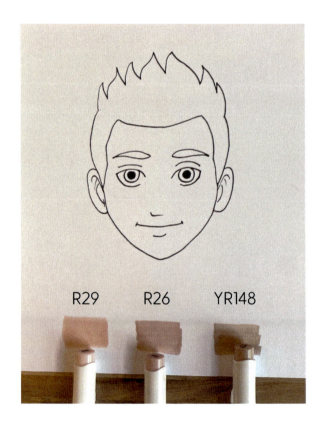

Step 1: Choose your palette. You can choose any palette from this book; they were chosen because they work. For this example, I'm choosing the following colors for my palette:

R29 - Pear Color
R26 - Honey
YR148 - Thin Persimmon

Make sure you ALWAYS test your markers before you begin on a piece of scratch paper to TRIPLE check that all the colors are what they seem and so there are NO surprises after you start.

You'll thank me for this later!

COLORING FIRST LAYERS

Step 2: Sweep the lightest color over the entire face.

There are no steadfast rules on how to get a large area covered. You can do a series of lines or move in a small circular motion. Your goal is simply to get the entire area covered WITHOUT doing any second layers yet.

Just a nice even coat over the whole thing. To make this the process go more quickly, I use the **SIDE of my brush nib.**

The brush nib is very agile and flexible. Changing how I hold the angle of the brush as I color, allows me to use the tip to nimbly navigate around the eye areas without having to pick up my marker.

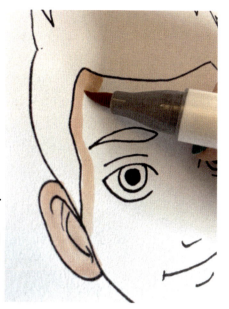

By contrast, the chisel nib is rather large and you have to pick it up off the paper many more times in order to get everything colored which results in more uneven areas of color.

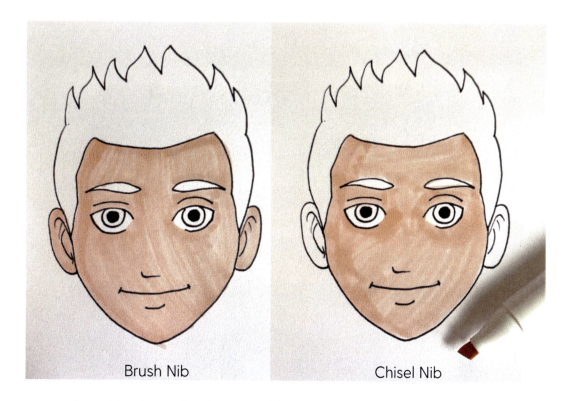

Brush Nib   Chisel Nib

Streaking is perfectly normal for the first layer, so don't panic!
Use the brush nib for an easier coloring process with fewer inconsistent areas.

COLORING SECOND LAYERS

Step 3: Use the second shade (in this case R26 - Honey) to add shading. We will cover shading and where to go with the darker colors in a moment. For now, let's just focus on coloring how to blend two (and then three) shades together nicely.

You can see it's still pretty choppy looking!

Again, I can't stress enough how normal that is!

Everything is fixable because unlike other markers, alcohol markers are BLENDABLE!

In order for us to blend colors together, we have to put them down first so all we need to next is keep on adding those colors!

On to the next step!

Step 4: Use the third (and darkest) shade (in this case YR148 - Thin Persimmon) to add additional shading. When you add darker shades, always make sure the area you cover is SMALLER than the first shaded area. So there is still plenty of the second (or medium or middle) shade showing. Like this:

See how the DARKEST color covers the SMALLEST area?

If you accidentally made the third (and darkest shade) area too large and covered up the second shade, you can even go back and enlarge the 2nd area again! No biggie :)

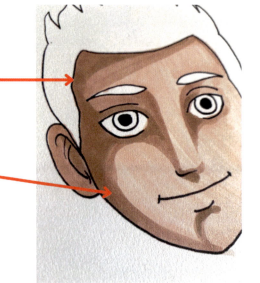

Still streaky, I know! We are about to take care of that in Step 5!

BLENDING IT ALL TOGETHER

Step 5: Now comes the fun blendy part! Go back to your lightest color. Sweep a layer over the ENTIRE face again. This time, pay careful attention to using strokes that go in the opposite direction as your first ones.

My first layer of R29 was layered with vertical strokes.

My second coat of R29 was put down horizontally.

A HUGE reduction in streaking!

 +  =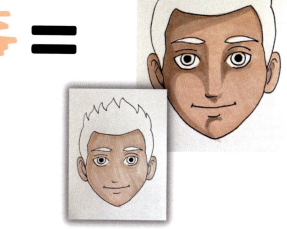

Tips: Again, use the SIDE of that flexy nib to sweep over the area swiftly. Use consistent pressure, and one clean pass, until the entire face is covered again.

You may notice how cold the paper is as you travel from one area of the face to the other.

That's the alcohol solution working its blending magic on the colors and pigments underneath! Okay, it's really just because it's wet again but still! It's so cool to know what is going on underneath your fingertips!!

After you give your paper a few moments to dry, you'll see the magical transformation! Your layers are blended and the streaks are significantly reduced!

TWEAKING FOR MORE DRAMA

Step 6: Now is the fun part! You get to tweak the skin tone to your liking. I'll point out here what all your options are and you can keep them in mind for all your future projects. The best part is that there are no rules! Only YOU get to decide how smooth you want your shading transitions to be. How much drama you create by adding more contrast or MORE highlights is up to you! So fun! So let's cover them here.

If you want an even smoother transition

Let's say you don't love the transitions from one shade to another. You still find that too jarring. What can you do?

Easy! Just add additional layers of the lightest color. Sweeping them over and over again until all the layers blend out better for you. Keep altering your directionality as you do so. This will only continue to help ease that transition and eliminate any streaking. If you don't want to darken the skin at all, just grab a marker that is ONE SHADE lighter than your first color.

You'll notice the colored areas will be darker when wet. Not to worry, they lighten as the paper dries again!

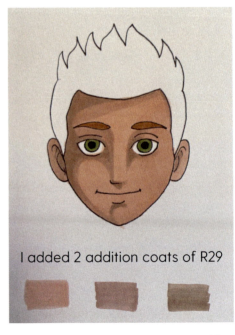

I added 2 addition coats of R29

ADDITIONAL TWEAKS
IF YOU WANT EVEN MORE DRAMA

Adding drama is super fun and easy! All the drama (no matter WHAT your drawing subject is!) comes from how sharp your contrast is! That means darks get DARKER and highlights are added to help to make things POP!

First, let's address the DARKS. Highlights I'm saving for last because they are the MOST FUN!! But last also because they are always the very last detail as they go on TOP of your previous layers.

So, if we want to go darker that means we need to pick out a 4th shade. Not to worry; just refer to the swatch pages and choose 1 shade DARKER in the SAME color family.

That means if you were working with PINK shades for the face (like this one) you want to pick a color that is DARK but also in the PINK family.

Looking at my swatch pages, I can see that **R27 - Pale Mauve** looks like a pretty good, darker choice in a similar color family. Now you simply add a touch of that in the same areas that we did for the other darker shades! But this time, keep that area even SMALLER than the areas applied to before! If you run out of room, quickly go back in with your first two shades and make those areas larger, so you have room for your 4th skin tone shade.

There's another trick to adding a 4th shade. Turn the page and I'll share with you what that is!

THE MASHING OF 4 LAYERS
MAKING THAT 4TH LAYER WORK

If you've gone ahead and added a 4th color to your face and now you're having a heart attack because it looks WAY TOO DARK and you're sweating and starting to REALLY freak out that you've ruined your drawing - RELAX. You've got this!!! Fixing that is easy peasy.

We decided to punch up our drawing and add a 4th color to the mix. But now it looks too dark. To fix, simply widen the areas of the colors 2 (R26) and 3 (YR148) and blend them again with color 1 (R29). Use multiple layers of color 2 (R26) to blend the areas over the new, larger, darker shaded region, much like we do when we blend the whole face with color 1 (R29).

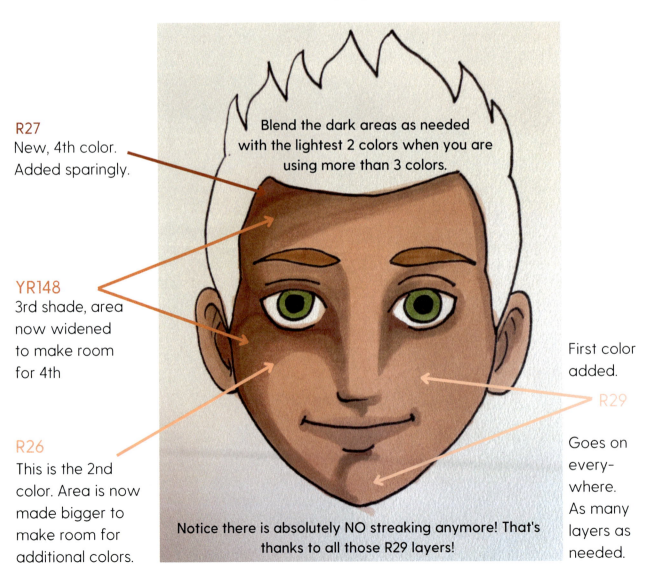

R27 New, 4th color. Added sparingly.

YR148 3rd shade, area now widened to make room for 4th

R26 This is the 2nd color. Area is now made bigger to make room for additional colors.

Blend the dark areas as needed with the lightest 2 colors when you are using more than 3 colors.

First color added.

R29 Goes on everywhere. As many layers as needed.

Notice there is absolutely NO streaking anymore! That's thanks to all those R29 layers!

ADJUSTING THE COLOR TINT
HOW TO CHANGE A BAD COLOR COMBO

Another common color scenario is that your face drawing looks too red, too yellow, too orange or just too SOMETHING. Do you have to scrap your drawing altogether? Heck no! One thing I've learned over the course of my creative career is that there is almost ALWAYS something you can do to save a piece of art from ending up in the bin!

Here's the easy workaround if your skin tone is too much of one color for your liking. Simply pick a LIGHT color from a DIFFERENT color family and give it a big sweep over the whole piece (much like we do to blend with the lightest color).

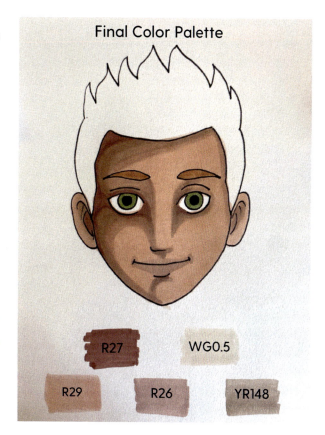

I'm taking the time to teach you all of these subtle variations and tricks because I know after so many years of teaching, sooooo many are too quick to give up when the going gets tough or when things don't turn out the way you hoped or had expected.

Hopefully you'll see there are always fun things you can try. Quite often these fixes really do work and you can make art that you can be truly proud of!

I also want you to know you can ADD more colors to the palettes you see in this book. Don't limit yourself! Make your own combinations too; be brave and try new things!

So in this instance, the face is a bit too pink for me (it looks more so in person than here). I grabbed my WG0.5 Warm Grey (as it's a very light, very neutral shade) to see if I could knock off some of the pinkiness of it!

Does it work? That is hard to tell, especially in this photo. But sweeping lighter colors over your face drawings can never hurt and will only act to blend blend blend. Definitely try this if you need help adjusting your colors. You may just be surprised!

FINISHING UP THE FEATURES
HELP RENDERING HAIR

All right, so we have covered making smooth skin tones, now let's finish up this guy before moving on to highlights and light sources. I already added eye color and some indication of lips. On guys, I just use a darker skin tone (rather than a pink color) so he doesn't look like he's wearing lipstick! Not that there's anything wrong with a guy wearing lipstick ;)

Pick out some hair color, and, like skin tones, 2-4 shades of one color is best! There is no one way to color hair. Just try different techniques and have fun with it and you'll be discovering your favorite ways and styles in no time!

Our dude friend we've been coloring all day has a hair shape that reminds me of flames so I kinda went with that look! I mean, why not?!

I chose 4 colors that went with each other. Two Copics and two from the Ohuhu skin tone pack. All alcohol markers work the same way, remember? So it's totally cool to mix and match your marker brands, as long as the ink inside is the same.

In small areas, start with the brush tip at the very start of the hair line. Keep hairs in the direction of the style or growth.

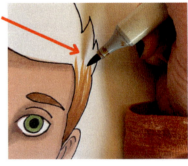

Then PULL upwards and release the nib. Keep the directionality of your marker the same for the whole movement. This gives the illusion of a hair strand.

All hair (regardless of style) looks most awesome if you render it from root to tip. Whether it's worn up, like on this guy, or down (like on my next example).

MORE HAIR HELP
USE THE BRUSH NIB "FLICK" TECHNIQUE - IT WORKS!

Just like when we color the skin from light to dark, we can do the same for the hair. We also keep the proportions of the lightest - darkest the same as well. So there will be the most of the light color showing and the least of the darkest.

Continue with the lightest shade until most of the hair space is filled in. I didn't realize I wanted to add the yellow tips until after I was finished so that's why I am starting with this color first.

Using the side of the nib makes drawing hair super fast!

Add the darkest colors last. Again, leaving the first layers exposed and going from the root and always flicking up with that brush nib.

When it's mostly all rendered, add the darkest color. ALWAYS start back at the roots when drawing hair (with one exception - turn page to see). I added the yellow at the end just for kicks. Now that you know how to render strands quickly and easily you can make any hairstyle look good!

HAIR HAIR AND MORE HAIR

ROOT TO TIP OR TIP TO ROOT?

As previously mentioned, that root-to-tip brush nib "flicking technique" can also be used on other hairstyles. Here are some good examples from some of my favorite drawings. In order to create the "highlighted" look in these examples, we use the same technique but with a twist :)

As you can see, there are three shades of purple working together here. But here I applied the technique TWICE. Once, to complete the root to tip look. And then again at the bottom. This time going tip to root!!

So no matter which direction you start, you NEVER draw a strand of hair starting from the middle. It should always be drawn from one of the two ends. Flick your way either up or down (or around a curve, as the style dictates because remember too: **directionality matters!**)

Make sure you curve your lines as the style dictates!

Not into all this flicking and highlighting business? No problem!! Take those same 2-4 shades of color and simply alternate them as you draw strands from root to tip - at any length you choose! And DONE!

TIPS FOR RENDERING WAVY HAIR

Rendering wavy hair is super fun and easy once you know how. Using the side of the brush nib for each strand also means you can render a full head of wavy hair in mere minutes! Just remember the "root to tip" philosophy and grab 3 or more colors that relate to one another. For this example I chose 2 Copics and 1 Ohuhu. Of course, I tested them first to make sure the combo would work well :)

Step 1: Pick at least 3 colors from the same color family.

Step 2: Start with the lightest shade. Using the SIDE of the brush nib, draw long, wavy strands from root to tip.

Be sure to still leave lots of room for the other colors. Wavy lines should mirror the wavy outside shape of the hair.

Step 3: Repeat with middle shade. Still be sure to leave some room for the third color!

Step 4: Repeat with darkest shade. If there are any white areas left you can repeat the other colors until the white of the paper is all filled in.

Done!

Step 5 (optional): Add some loose strands with a fine liner and/or white highlights with a paint marker!

TIPS FOR RENDERING TIGHT CURLS
YOU'VE GOT OPTIONS!

I love playing around to create different types of curly hair. Here are 3 ways to create fun tight curly hairstyles. Have a go at each kind to see which one you like best!

ONE Step Hair Effect

All it takes to create this effect is a single shade of marker and lots of squiggly lines!

The trick is to leave little spots of the paper showing through!

TWO Step Hair Effect

With a light color, fill in the entire hair area with squiggly small circles.
Then repeat squiggles with a slightly darker shade, leaving lots of the first color exposed.

THREE Step Hair Effect

First, use the brush nib of 3-4 colors to "stamp" marks until the entire hair area is colored in. Then add black & white squiggles.

NOW ONTO SHADING!

One of the coolest ways to add dimension to a face drawing is to render shading accurately. We have already gone through one example but I didn't give you any reasoning WHY I was adding shading to the places that I did. We are going to unpack that here :) Below is a portrait. As you can see, there is a shadow over the left side of her face.

Sometimes it is easier to understand shading and values when they are in black and white, hence the two versions.

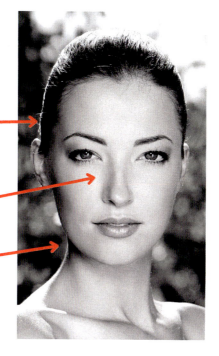

Can you see how much darker this side of the face is?

And along the left side of her nose?

And under her chin/neck on this side?

The left side is IN SHADOW because there is a strong light source that is coming from the right hand side. The shadow is always opposite the lightsource.

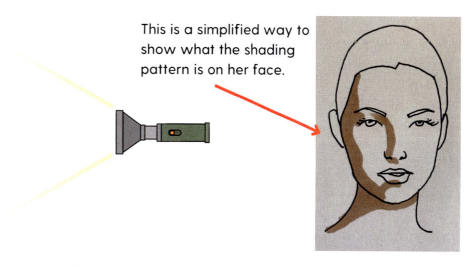

This is a simplified way to show what the shading pattern is on her face.

Knowing WHERE common shading patterns occur on a face and then being able to render them with some degree of accuracy is...well it's awesome!! And it's just what will take YOUR drawings to the next level!

LIGHT SOURCES CONTINUED.

A face can have a subtle shadow (like in the first example), or a strong and seemingly dramatic one (like in this example here). In both cases, however, the shadow patterns are essentially the same.

Remind you of anyone? Now you know where my idea came from!

In addition to showing you the coordinating skin tone colors in this Guide, I also want to teach you about shading because it's how you make your faces come to life. I've made it SUPER EASY for you in this book. All you have to do is look at the examples, shown below, and then follow the 3 easy steps as shown on each page of each section to take to get there!

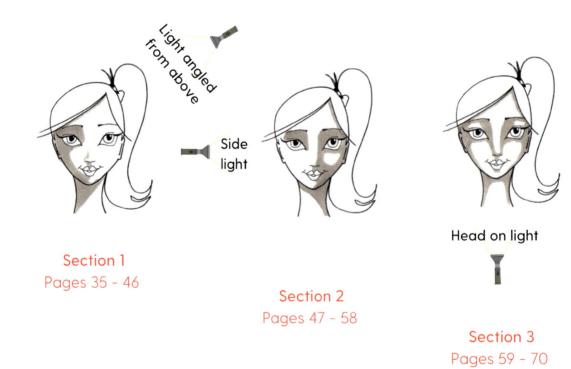

Section 1
Pages 35 - 46

Section 2
Pages 47 - 58

Section 3
Pages 59 - 70

Just as a reminder: you can freely mix and match any of the skin tones in this Guide with any shading patterns you see throughout each of the three sections!

It makes SUCH an impact on your drawings!! And it's super easy once you know how.

NOW...HIGHLIGHTS

I cannot write a book about shadows and not talk about the highlights!! Besides, they are the most fun of ALL!! I always use a white paint marker for this task (see page 4 for my favorite brands). A gel pen NEVER quite gets it done to my satisfaction. I like my highlights to be brash and bold and not shy, sketchy little things!

Below is a mixed media project I created for my students at Awesome Art School. At the end of the lesson, I added highlights to all of the possible places one can. To be clear: **I don't use this many in one project but I wanted to teach you EXACTLY all the places you COULD.** Pick and choose as you please! Generally just a few is enough.

On dudes, I limit highlights to pupils and maybe just a dash on the nose/chin!

On individual hair strands.

On corner of forehead where light source may hit. Also center of forehead.

On the brow bone is lovely.

Pops also look pretty on the eye-lid (top or bottom), iris, pupil, on lid and in the tear duct.

Top of ear (or where light source tags) and a spot (or area) on the upper cheekbone.

On the ball of the nose. Up the nose bridge.

Nostrils, cupid bow, top of upper lip.

Ball of the chin and lower lip.

WHAT NOT TO USE WITH ALCOHOL MARKERS

As I'm a mixed media artist by trade (that means I love to mash loads of art supplies together in a single project), I know all too well some of you will want to add other mediums to your drawings too. That's cool! BUT...there are some rules you need to follow to get the best results. Unlike water-based markers and art supplies (that make up the lion's share of the arts and crafts market), alcohol-based inks and markers, unfortunately, don't play nicely with others.

So, as much as it's super FUN to mix and match all your supplies together, you can't really do that with alcohol markers without suffering some pretty big (and not so awesome) consequences.

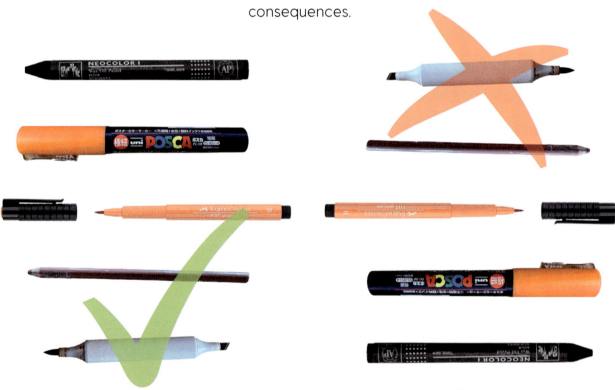

Alcohol Markers can play host to many other dry mediums (as long as the new mediums sit on TOP of the alcohol ink).

But you should not layer Alcohol Markers OVER other mediums.
They really only play well with other alcohol ink products (or as a base layer).

Colored pencils and other inks do pair beautifully OVER alcohol markers and you can get some insanely beautiful results by doing so! I highly recommend playing around with pencils on top of your marker face drawings some time if you've never tried it!

HOW COLORS ARE SELECTED

The first step (as always) is to test each color in the 36 (or 24) piece set. Unfortunately, the order on the swatch card (that comes with the set) isn't very helpful.

Visually (at least for me) it's super difficult to see which colors go together. So the next thing I do is to regroup the colors into color families that make sense to my brain :)

I sort the colors into 4 color families: yellows, neutrals, red/pink and peach/orange.

I literally cut up my swatches into squares and lay them out so I can really see which ones go toghether. Ahhhhhh, this is so much better.

I highly recommend you try this with ANY art supply you have when it comes to creating skin tones!

Sooooo extraordinarily helpful!

YELLOW SHADES

As you can see, the true colors don't always match the name the manufacturer gives to them. Once you have your colors in color-family categories, you can always safely pick your 2-4 shades quickly and easily!

Most humans don't have yellow skin. Used straight from the palette these colors are perfect for cartoon characters though (think the Simpsons!).

PINK/RED SHADES

Careful using all colors from this category! Using ALL red shades can definitely give the appearance of a sunburn. For baby drawings, you can sometimes get away with it!

30

BROWNS/NEUTRALS

These are the "safe" color choices. When you don't want a too yellow or a too orange or a too sunburned look, grab colors from here and you'll be good to go every time!

PEACH/ORANGES

Interestingly, the colors in the top row make a great choice for almost all light and medium skin tone combinations. Note: Terra Cotta made its way to two groupings. That's because the jump from Salmon to Chestnut brown was just too great. Terra Cotta DOES have a lot of orange in it and would pair beautifully between Salmon and Chestnut Brown so in it goes!

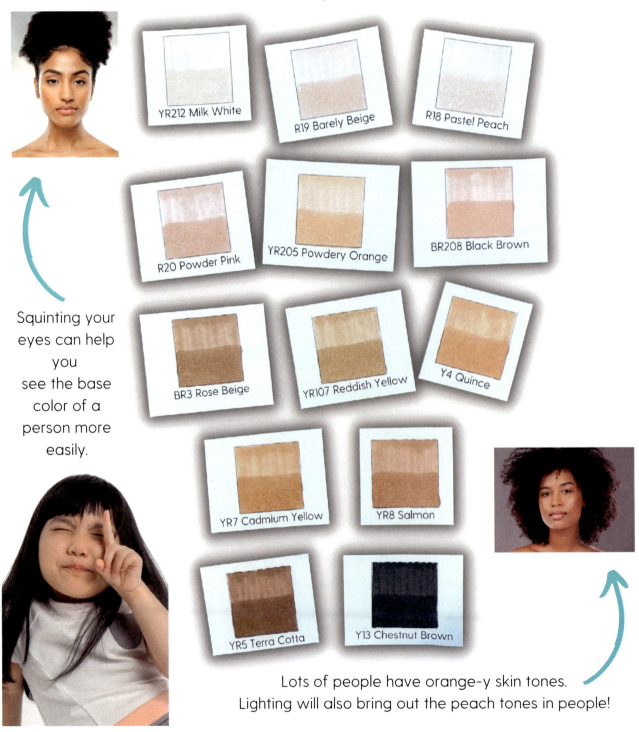

Squinting your eyes can help you see the base color of a person more easily.

Lots of people have orange-y skin tones. Lighting will also bring out the peach tones in people!

- YR212 Milk White
- R19 Barely Beige
- R18 Pastel Peach
- R20 Powder Pink
- YR205 Powdery Orange
- BR208 Black Brown
- BR3 Rose Beige
- YR107 Reddish Yellow
- Y4 Quince
- YR7 Cadmium Yellow
- YR8 Salmon
- YR5 Terra Cotta
- Y13 Chestnut Brown

HOW TO USE THIS BOOK

The most GORGEOUS skin tones are created by combining colors ACROSS color families though, not just within them. Luckily I've done all the choosing for you. All YOU have to do is pick one and go!

Step One: You create your drawing. It can be from your imagination or from a reference or from one of my drawing books!

Step Two: Figure out which shading pattern you want to create on your drawing. Remember: this book features three of the most common ones typically seen in nature/photography:

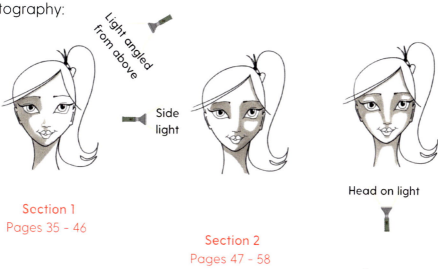

Section 1
Pages 35 - 46

Section 2
Pages 47 - 58

Section 3
Pages 59 - 70

Step Three: Flip through the book and pick out any skin tone combination you like!

R26 Honey

R27 Pale Mauve

R28 Colocasia Tonoimo

Step Four: Grab your markers and follow the step-by-step directions on each page so you know just where to go with your darks and lights! Et VOILA!

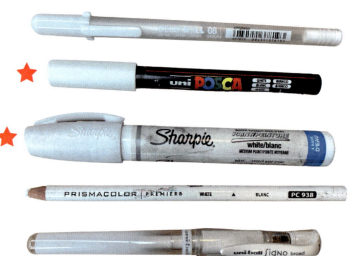

Step Five: Bust out your creativity when deciding on hair and eye colors, accessories and details!

Need help with highlights? Refer back to page 27 or any of the colored examples in this book, as needed, for creative places to put those fun POPS of white!

*my favorites!

How to use this book if you don't own Ohuhu's? I have made a 12 page resource guide that is a color and color family comparison of all the Copic, Ohuhu and Arteza Everblend Alcohol Marker Skin Tone colors (Copics has over 130 skin tone colors!!!). If you have **any** of these brands you can use my guide to choose comparable colors that appear in THIS book! Best part? It's free!! Just type in this link (carefully) and I'll email it right over!

https://awesomeartschool.lpages.co/skin-tone-marker-guide/

SECTION 1 - LIGHT TOP LEFT OR TOP RIGHT

SIMPLIFIED VIEW

REAL-WORLD EXAMPLES

These are all valid examples!! Are they not?!

I hope this is helpful!

WG0.5 Warm Grey 0

+ YR212 Milk White

+ Barely Beige

TO FINISH THE LOOK:

Add cheeks with R21 Fruit Pink. Doesn't get much cuter than this!!!

YR212 Milk White

+ R18 Pastel Peach

+ R19 Barely Beige

TO FINISH THE LOOK:

This is a great skin tone combination when you don't want too much contrast or the character you are creating as super pale skin.

Want to kick your shading up a notch? Add R20 Powder Pink to the mix!

TO FINISH THE LOOK:

Adding light-colored eyes to a darker skin tone palette is a fun way to spice up an otherwise more "hum drum" character!

R26 Honey

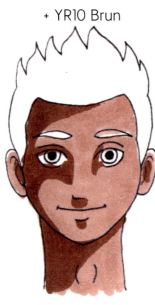

+ YR10 Brun

+ YR91 Natural Oak

scans

photos

You can see how much the scanning process alters the true colors of the ink!
That's why testing your own markers is so important.

WG0.5 Warm Grey 0

+ R19 Barely Beige

+ R29 Pear Color

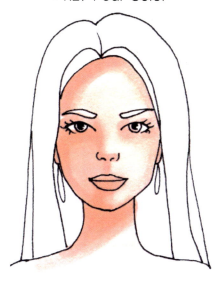

TO FINISH THE LOOK:

These three colors really blend seamlessly together. Want to add pink cheeks? Consider R21 Fruit Pink...or R20 Power Pink! Yes, either works!

R29 Pear Color

+ R26 Honey

+ R27 Pale Mauve

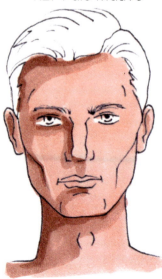

TO FINISH THE LOOK:

If streaking is a problem then go over the entire face a few times with a LIGHTer color. A lighter color will also help cut down on the "sunburnt" appearance.

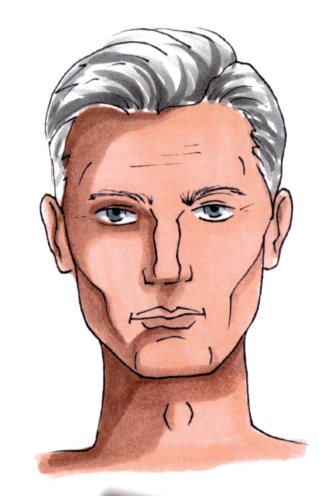

R18 Pastel Peach

+ YR20 Morin

+ R27 Pale Mauve

To Finish the Look:

Add the illusion of cheekbones by sweeping YR20 Morin on either side of the face. Use a white paint marker to add highlights to the nose bridge, lower lip, chin and eyes!

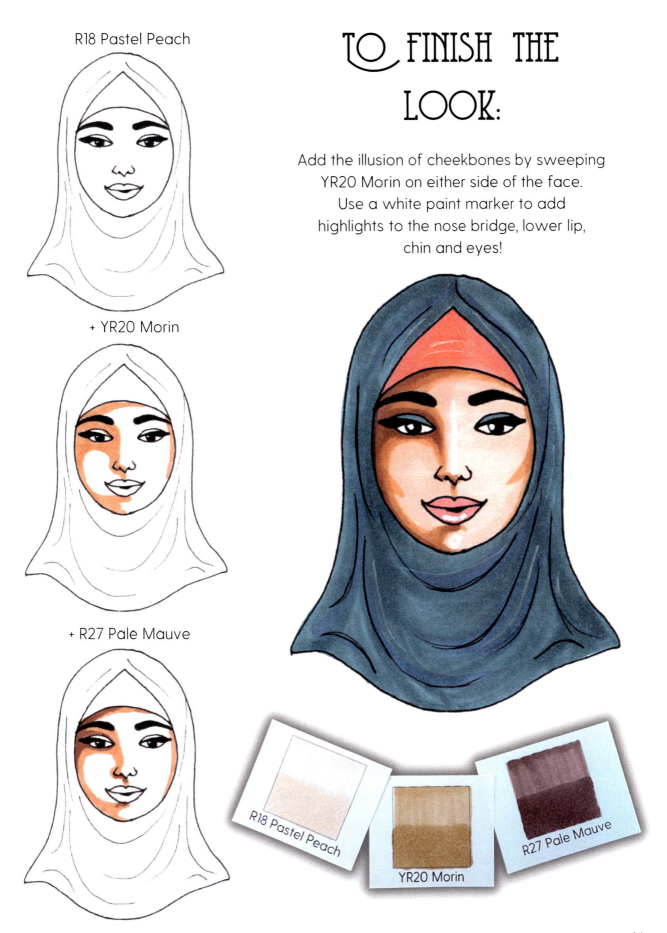

R18 Pastel Peach

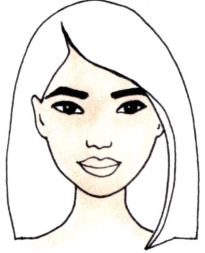

+ R29 Pear Color

+ R26 Honey

TO FINISH THE LOOK:

Sweep a second layer of R18 Pastel Peach over the entire left side of face and forehead. Then add that same color to the right side but ONLY around eye and along the right side along the hairline. Keep the nose bridge and chin untouched.

YR209 Hazelnuts

+ BR2 Potato Brown

+ YR91 Natural Oak

To Finish the Look:

To create the illusion of dramatic hair highlights, leave an area across the center of the bangs with no color at all.
Use a white paint marker to add highlights to the left brow ridge, nose tip, and lower lip!

YR212 Milk White

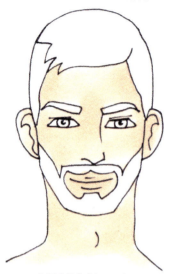

+ YR209 Hazelnuts

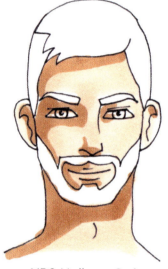

+ YR9 Yellow Ochre

TO FINISH THE LOOK:

When there is facial hair involved, the shadows still fall consistently according to the light source. So if the light is on the right, the left side (under the beard and neck) will be in shadow.

YR20 Morin

+ BR2 Potato Brown

+ YR10 Brun

TO FINISH THE LOOK:

By keeping the center of the eyelids the white of the paper (or adding highlights afterwards with a white paint pen) you create the look of gorgeous made-up eye-lids!

The hair is simply various shades of wavy black and brown lines from root to tip.

Y9 Yellow Ochre

+ Y10 Brun

+ YR91 Natural Oak

TO FINISH THE LOOK:

After the third color layer, go back and add another layer of the lightest, Y9 Yellow Ochre. Make sure you vary your strokes with each subsequent layer and you'll eliminate any streakiness!

SECTION 2 - LIGHT LEFT OR RIGHT

SIMPLIFIED VIEW

REAL-WORLD EXAMPLES

R30 Pale Cherry Pink

+ R21 Fruit Pink

+ BR208 Black Brown

TO FINISH THE LOOK:

If by chance your Br208 IS a real brown/black, then you can grab your Y4 Quice or YR205 Powdery Orange for the same effect.

R30 Pale Cherry Pink

R21 Fruit Pink

BR208 Black Brown

YR205 Powdery Orange

Y4 Quince

R19 Barely Beige

+ R29 Pear Color

+ BR3 Rose Beige

TO FINISH THE LOOK:

While the jump from Pear Color to Rose Beige looks like a big one, the result is just stunning. Be creative when you mix your skin tones, you may just be pleasantly surprised!

R18 Pastel Peach

+ YR205 Powdery Orange

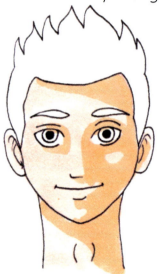

+ YR107 Reddish Yellow

To finish the look:

If you're in doubt about an overall skin tone, make the hair in similar colors and suddenly it all comes together!

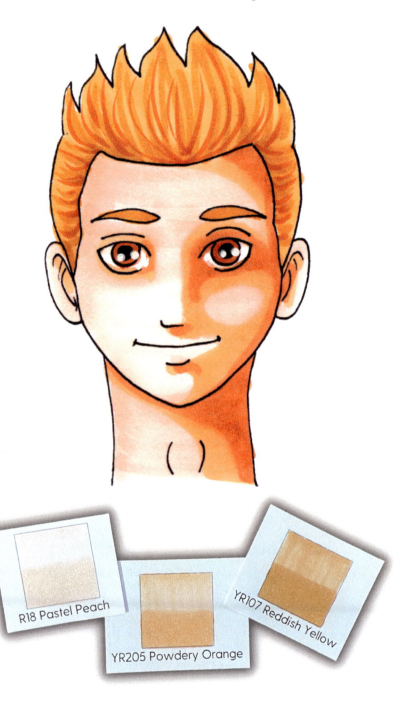

R29 Pear Color

+ R26 Honey

TO FINISH THE LOOK:

Adding details like white streaks in the hair and freckles make her really come to life!

+ YR148 Thin Persimmon

R18 Pastel Peach

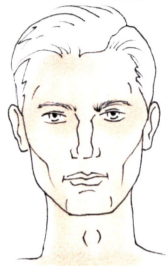

+ Y20 Morin

+ Y145 Buttercup Yellow

TO FINISH THE LOOK:

If you'd like to add even darker darks, reach for BR2 - it goes perfectly with the first three!

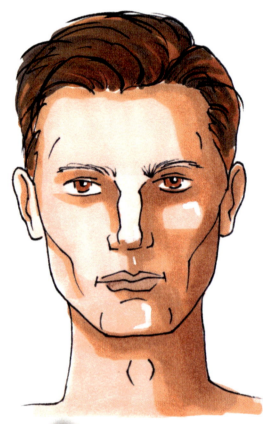

WG0.5 Warm Grey 0

TO FINISH THE LOOK:

WG0.5 is a perfect neutral. Go over all of the layers and shades a lot of times to get this streak free look.

+ R29 Pear Color

+ R26 Honey

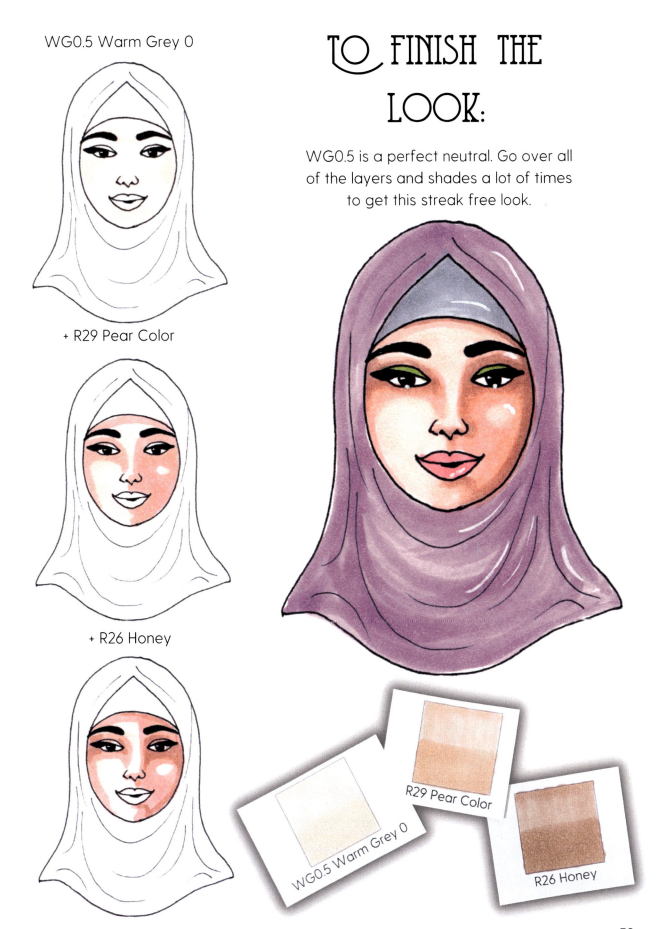

YR20 Morin

+ Y145 Buttercup Yellow

+ Y12 Mahogany

TO FINISH THE LOOK:

Shades of grey for hair look just as awesome as any other color so don't be afraid to go there :) Want to go deeper with shading? YR95 Burnt Sienna pairs well with this grouping.

Y9 Yellow Ochre

+ Y12 Mahogany

+ YR92 Chocolate

TO FINISH THE LOOK:

Don't be afraid to use super dark colors! They look absolutely gorgeous together and, coupled with bright white highlights, always looks just WOW!

YR20 Morin

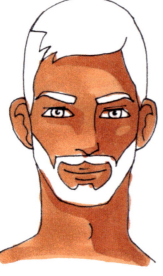

+ BR3 Rose Beige

+ Y12 Mahogany

TO FINISH THE LOOK:

Add a second coat of YR20 Morin just to the right-shaded side and around and left eye for a more dramatic impact without making the entire face darker.

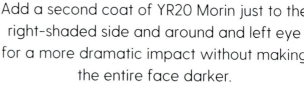

YR20 Morin

BR3 Rose Beige

Y12 Mahagany

Y145 Buttercup Yellow

+ YR9 Yellow Ochre

+ Y12 Mahogany

To Finish the Look:

An easy way to create the look of flowing hair is to color the base a solid color and then simply run individual strands of black and white from root to tip.

Y145 Buttercup Yellow

Y9 Yellow Ochre

Y12 Mahagany

57

YR107 Reddish Brown

+ YR5 Terra Cotta

+ YR91 Natural Oak

TO FINISH THE LOOK:

Contrast dark skin with fun, bright and lighter colors for the hair, lips and eyeshadow. Soooooo fun!

YR107 Reddish Yellow
YR5 Terra Cotta
YR91 Natural Oak

SECTION 3 - LIGHT HEAD ON

SIMPLIFIED VERSION

Sorry!
I couldn't resist!

REAL-WORLD

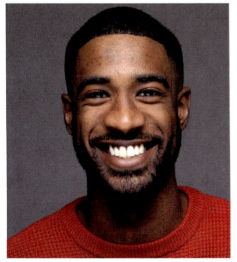

Just look for the symmetry.
Once you see it, it's hard to
un-see it!
(And that's a good thing)!

EXAMPLES!

SO FUN!

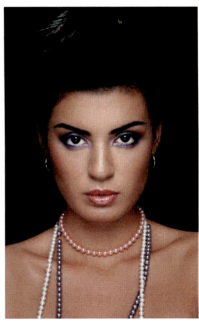

R30 Pale Cherry Pink

+ R26 Honey

+ YR9 Yellow Ochre

TO FINISH THE LOOK:

Use a light, neutral shade like WG0.5 Warm Grey 0 to blend all the colors together without creating a sunburnt look on your sweet baby :)

R30 Pale Cherry Pink

R26 Honey

YR9 Yellow Ochre

R18 Pastel Peach

+ R29 Pear Color

+ R26 Honey

To Finish the Look:

Adding a touch of white to the lower eye lid makes the eyes look like they're sparkling!

Y121 Primrose

+ YR6 Primary Yellow

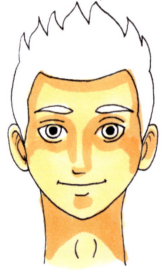

+ YR34 Yellow

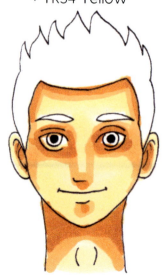

TO FINISH THE LOOK:

This color palette definitely has a Simpson vibe but it works as the colors all relate to one another so perfectly!

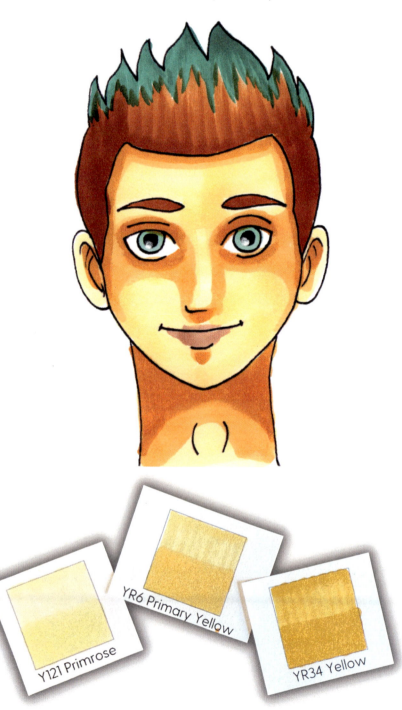

62

R29 Pear Color

+ R26 Honey

+ R27 Pale Mauve

To Finish the Look:

Don't have a white paint pen? You can just as easily create the illusion of a highlight by simply leaving the white of the paper showing.

Y20 Morin

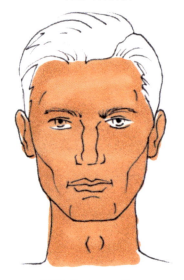

+ BR2 Potato Brown

+ YR10 Natural Oak

TO FINISH THE LOOK:

If you want to add more nuance to your shading, you can do layers of the lightest color but SKIP areas you want to keep lighter like the forehead, nose and chin.

YR20 Morin — BR2 Potato Brown — YR91 Natural Oak

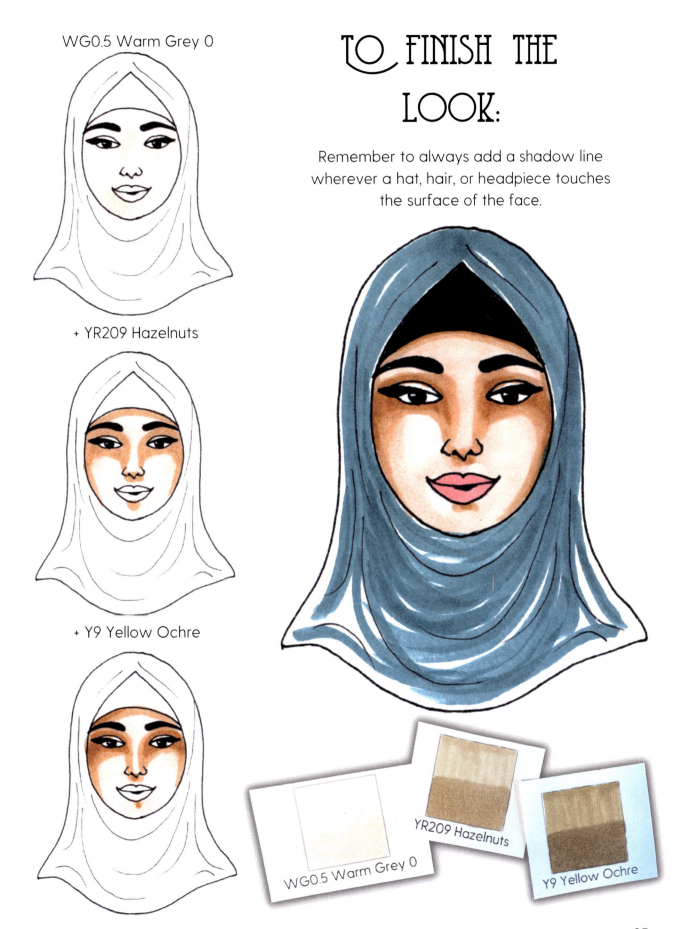

R29 Pear Color

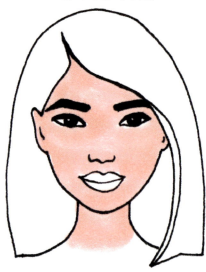

To Finish the Look:

Add a single strand of color in an otherwise boring hairstyle or color to add a dash of excitement!

+ YR148 Thin Persimmon

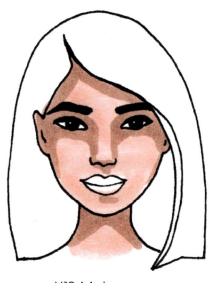

+ Y12 Mahogany

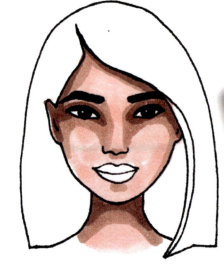

R29 Pear Color · YR148 Thin Persimmon · Y12 Mahagany

YR107 Reddish Yellow

+ BR3 Rose Beige

+ BR2 Potato Brown

TO FINISH THE LOOK:

Drawing hair as if the marker strokes were actual hair strands will add realism to your faces!

YR107 Reddish Yellow · BR3 Rose Beige · BR2 Potato Brown

BR2 Potato Brown

+ YR91 Natural Oak

+ Y13 Chestnut Brown

To Finish the Look:

With this dark skin tone combination, it is a good idea to go over the shaded regions with the BR2 Potato Brown to blend. Leave the forehead and nose bridge alone though. That will create a nice light contrast.

R26 Honey

+ R27 Pale Mauve

+ R28 Colocasia Tonoimo

TO FINISH THE LOOK:

Contrast dark skin with light hair and bright bold highlights for a super fun effect!!!

R26 Honey

R27 Pale Mauve

R28 Colocasia Tonoimo

Y12 Mahogany

+ R28 Colocasia Tonoimo

+ YR95 Burnt Sienna

TO FINISH THE LOOK:

Colors that have similar values will create a less dramatic contrast. Sometimes less is more and that's okay!

OTHER USES FOR THIS BOOK!

So you purchased this book only to find out you can get ahold of the same markers. Now what? Did you waste your money? No way, Jose! Here's why:

1-2-3 COLOR SELECTION THEORY HOLDS

Whether you are working in markers of any kind, colored pencils, acrylics or watercolors, or ANY OTHER medium you love, the concept of choosing 3 colors in the same color family to render skin tones remains the same. You can use your eye to match up the colors in this book to the colors of the mediums you are already using to create fantastic skin tones at any time! Play and test and you'll soon discover your favorite mixes in your favorite mediums! YES! You can DO THIS! This Guide will give you the confidence to try.

Look for skin tone sets in all your favorite mediums to help you too!! You'd be surprised at how easy brands are making it to help you get creative and have success when rendering people and faces! Swatch them out, choose your shades and give it a go!

UNIVERSAL SHADING PRINCIPLES

As you've hopefully learned after reading this Guide, knowing exactly WHERE to shade (and WHY) is key to creating skin tones that make SENSE when you are looking at a drawn or painted face. Just as with color selection, you can refer back to these shading principles and illustrations of shading patterns to help you render amazing skin tones every time you draw and color a face in ANY of your favorite mediums and marker brands! And by golly this is art, so HAVE FUN WITH IT!!!

 # FREEBIES!

Want to practice coloring and shading on actual faces? Yay! I made a fun 25-page PDF of the swatching squares that I use PLUS all the characters in this book for you to color! To grab the free download go to

https://create.awesomeartschool.com/drawing-face-coloring-sheets/

You can print them out on cardstock and practice your skin tones and color swatching! You can also use them to test out and invent new combinations of colors.

Find a new skin combo you HAVE to share?
I wanna hear about it!
Join me in my Facebook Group and tag me so I can see!
www.facebook.com/groups/awesomeartschool
or tag me on instagram! @karencampbellartist

And in case you missed it, I've also swatched the entire range of 136 Copic Skin Colors and compared them to both the 36 Ohuhu (the ones I feature in this Guide) and the 36 Arteza Everblend Skin Tone Sets so you can use this book with all your favorite alcohol marker brands!

To grab that 12 page PDF free resource go to:
https://awesomeartschool.lpages.co/skin-tone-marker-guide/

LET'S CONNECT!

 karencampbellartist.com (blog and info about art clubs)
awesomeartschool.com (official art school website)

 youtube.com/karencampbellartist (mixed media art)
youtube.com/karencampbellDRAWS (how to draw)

 facebook.com/karencampbellartist
facebook.com/groups/awesomeartschool (group)

 @karencampbellartist (personal/professional)
@awesomeartschool (this is where we feature students!)

 amazon.com/author/karencampbell (links to all my books)
amazon.com/shop/karencampbellartist
(links to my fave art supplies)

 etsy.com/shop/karencampbellartist

Karen Campbell
Artist, Author, Teacher

Karen Campbell is a Boston area native who lives in North Carolina with her husband, 3 kids and 4 fur babies. She started teaching art in 2011 and founded her online art school, Awesome Art School, in 2016.

Thanks to her school, many art books, and 2 YouTube Channels, Karen has had the pleasure of impacting the lives of tens of thousands of adult learners across the globe with fun art lessons.

Karen's primary goal is to make art easy and accessible to everyone. Besides techniques, she focuses her students' attention on becoming better artists through the practice of having pure, unadulterated FUN!!!

LET'S HAVE MORE FUN TOGETHER!

For more advanced drawing and marker FUN!

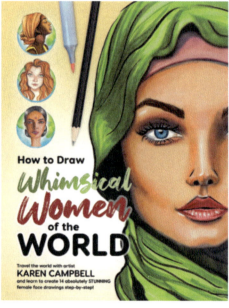

IF you're interested in learning to draw...from scratch! Figure book is coming soon!

This fun little series has lots of marker projects in it as well!

And to learn more about how to mix your mediums and painting techniques!

LET'S CONNECT!

 karencampbellartist.com (blog and info about art clubs)
awesomeartschool.com (official art school website)

 youtube.com/karencampbellartist (mixed media art)
youtube.com/karencampbellDRAWS (how to draw)

 facebook.com/karencampbellartist
facebook.com/groups/awesomeartschool (group)

 @karencampbellartist (personal/professional)
@awesomeartschool (this is where we feature students!)

 amazon.com/author/karencampbell (links to all my books)
amazon.com/shop/karencampbellartist
(links to my fave art supplies)

 etsy.com/shop/karencampbellartist

Karen Campbell
Artist, Author, Teacher

Karen Campbell is a Boston area native who lives in North Carolina with her husband, 3 kids and 4 fur babies. She started teaching art in 2011 and founded her online art school, Awesome Art School, in 2016.

Thanks to her school, many art books, and 2 YouTube Channels, Karen has had the pleasure of impacting the lives of tens of thousands of adult learners across the globe with fun art lessons.

Karen's primary goal is to make art easy and accessible to everyone. Besides techniques, she focuses her students' attention on becoming better artists through the practice of having pure, unadulterated FUN!!!

LET'S HAVE MORE FUN TOGETHER!

For more advanced drawing and marker FUN!

IF you're interested in learning to draw...from scratch! Figure book is coming soon!

This fun little series has lots of marker projects in it as well!

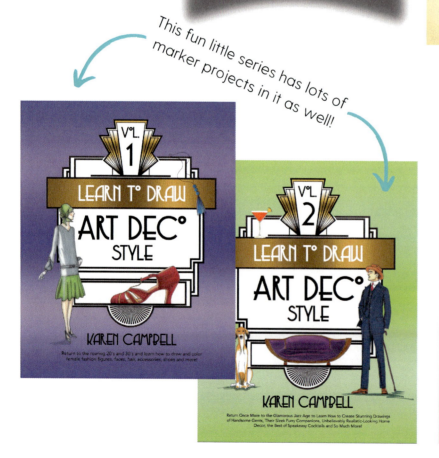

And to learn more about how to mix your mediums and painting techniques!

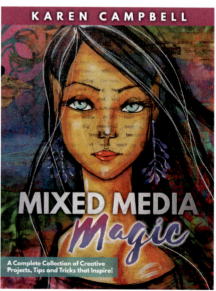

Made in the USA
Las Vegas, NV
08 May 2025

21872240R00045